Family Care
Westwood House

C is for **Confidence**

A Guide to Running Confidence Building Courses
for Women of All Ages

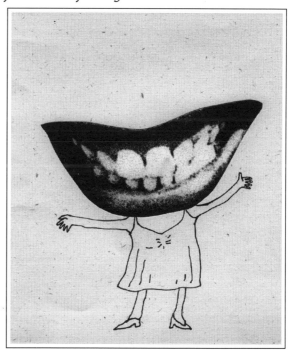

First published in 1998 by:
Women and New Directions, Edinburgh

Minor amendments incorporated in a
Second Edition published in 2001 by:
Russell House Publishing Ltd.
4 St. George's House
Uplyme Road
Lyme Regis
Dorset DT7 3LS

Tel: 01297-443948
Fax: 01297-442722
e-mail: help@russellhouse.co.uk

British Library Cataloguing-in-publication Data:

A catalogue record for this book is available from the British Library.

ISBN: 1-903855-02-0

Edited by Shirley Henderson
Additional editorial work for the second edition by Jenny Nemko
Designed by Trish Reeves, Greater Pilton Print Resource
Printed by Polestar, Exeter

About Russell House Publishing

RHP is a group of social work, probation, education and youth and
community work practitioners and academics working in collaboration with
a professional publishing team.
Our aim is to work closely with the field to produce innovative and valuable
materials to help managers, trainers, practitioners and students.
We are keen to receive feedback on publications and new ideas for future
projects.

Contents

Family Care
Westwood Hou...

Step by Step List of Exercises

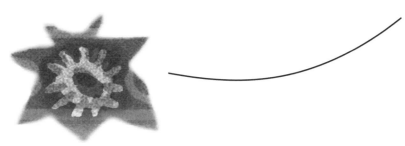

C is for **Confidence**

An Introduction

We believe that confidence is the foundation stone of personal development. Assertive behaviour can be learned and applied successfully ONLY when self esteem and personal confidence issues have been addressed. This realisation was arrived at after many years working with women, much of this time spent at Women And New Directions an urban aid project for women in Edinburgh. As confidence is a concept rather than a behaviour, it is impossible to define and difficult to explain. The only way to build it is to experience the empowering process. Now for the first time, we present some of the excercises we use in our training and development consultancy partnership, INSPIRE. We have developed a formula that will enable you to put together your own training course with the reassurance that all the materials have been tried and tested.

Mary Blair and Lesley Wilson are both qualified in Community Education and provide personal development training and consultancy services, with partner Pat Armstrong, through their Edinburgh-based business, Inspire (www.inspiretraining.co.uk).

C is for **C**onfidence

Helps you plan and organise your own confidence building course;

◉ Gives you a choice of really useful exercises;

◉ Encourages you to feel more confident as a facilitator;

◉ Identifies key readings which will develop your understanding of personal development for women.

How to use this manual

This manual has been designed as a "pick up and use" tool. Depending on your needs, you can follow our approach to confidence building from start to finish, or you can dip in and pull out exercises that are appropriate to your group. All exercises requiring handouts are set out on separate pages and can be easily photocopied.

Running Confidence Building Courses
Our Approach

We tell women, "This course will build your confidence." They say, "Yes! That's what we want." And it's true. Like everyone else, they want to feel better about themselves. But how do you go about helping people feel better about themselves?

The process is a conscious engaging of internal and external factors to a depth (different for each individual), which results in them changing their perception of themselves. This process is not complicated. But it is extremely delicate. It's like making good wine or a fresh soufflé. All the ingredients must combine at the right time and in the right quantities.

Working with people must be the most frustrating and rewarding job in the world. You can achieve results far beyond your expectations, but you cannot control the process. Things will not go as expected. Some people will emerge cooked to perfection. Others may be a little underdone or over done.

The process is not easy - for tutor or participants. The tutor's task is to develop a programme in which participants challenge themselves, taking each step in personal development as steadily as is comfortable for them. Undoubtedly, with each new group of participants, tutors take on a huge responsibility. But, we are not responsible for participants' lives. Our responsibility is to show them a selection of tools for building confidence. It is then their responsibility to choose what they want, and put them into use. Some will reject it all, saying it's not for them. But, they will leave with more than they came. Each experience, whether good or not so good, offers opportunities. Some will pick up everything they can carry, diving into self exploration with enthusiasm. They feel exhilarated, alive and eager to start afresh.

So how do we actually do this? We normally work with groups of eight to twelve women, running for two hours per week for ten weeks. We use a range of exercises and activities designed to be enjoyable and non-threatening which focus on individual experiences. The first stage is to encourage sharing. Isolation of thought and experience is the most powerful barrier to change. In a ten week course running for two hours per week, this stage may last from two to five weeks.

In stage two exercises are less emotional and less introspective. Participants begin to recognise the powerful tools they already have at their disposal. They begin to examine their lives, their roles in society and to question long-held perceptions. It is crucially important to give women space to flex their intellect. The women we have worked with are bright, clever, talented, creative and powerful, yet often they have no perception of those aspects of themselves.

In stage three we look at strategies. Women support each other in their plans. They have made connections and friends.

Ending a course is as important as the beginning. Women are more confident by the end. They feel more powerful, but are about to lose the support of weekly sessions with the group. They are reluctant to let go saying, "But what next?" However, by this time, they will have a bag of tools, some new friends, and several options to consider. WAND's philosophy is about moving on. To bring our service to as many women as possible, we need women to move on. And so, ending is turned into a celebration of what has been, and is yet to be accomplished.

Mary Blair and Lesley Wilson

An A to Z Guide to Running Confidence Building Courses

A is for Atmosphere and Anecdotes

As soon as women arrive, they need to have their worries dispelled. You can achieve this by working hard to make sure that the **a**TMOSPHERE in the venue is welcoming, non-threatening and empowering. It's all too easy to become accustomed to working in a dreary, badly maintained environment. So much so that you can forget what it must be like for women attending for the first time. For most people, the visual appearance accounts for 80% of their initial judgement about whether they like what they've come to. It is therefore essential, that any venue for this type of work must reach the highest standard. The training room should be bright and beautiful. Women are especially sensitive to colour and design, and if you can invest some time, money and creativity into making your venue look good, it will pay dividends. Sound is also extremely important. A draughty hall with no carpeting gives a hollow scary echo, so make sure that the sound levels are soft. You could have some music playing in the background as the women arrive. Smell can also play a huge part in first impressions, so why not try some aromatherapy oils, joss sticks, or brew some freshly made coffee? The comfort of carpet cushioning each step, as opposed to a hard floor sending shock vibrations up the spine, is also preferable. Soft furnishings, which caress your bottom rather than those awful grey or red hard plastic chairs, will also win you brownie points. The taste buds may be titillated with some biscuits. None of these ideas need cost a fortune. Creativity is the key. A final point about atmosphere: women will pick up on any subtle stress which you or your co-worker are experiencing so make sure that you get rid of it before your group begins.

Include any relevant stories that you may have experienced or heard when illustrating important points. Women like to hear about other women's successes and failures, and you should always encourage group members to contribute their own **a**NECDOTES, where appropriate.

B is for Books and Biscuits

BOOKS are an essential element of any confidence building course. They provide a stimulus for discussion and can be a useful tool in personal development. There are various authors writing about different aspects of confidence building, and it is up to each individual to find out whose style best suits them. You may not have the financial resources to supply each member with their own copy of a particular book, but you should encourage them to borrow books from the library, from each other and look out at car boot sales for cheaper copies!! We have suggested some of our favourites at the end of this manual.

BISCUITS are very, very popular and if your resources run to chocolate, then you're surely onto a winner!!

C is for Childcare, Coffee and Certificates

If you truly want to work with women then you need to provide **c**HILDCARE. Now the childcare which supplements the personal development and growth of women does not mean seven children in a cupboard with a very nice woman watching out for them. Childcare means a properly equipped crêche, which is light, bright and supervised by qualified childcare workers who enjoy their work and get paid a decent rate for the job. These elements are crucial for several reasons. Firstly, it is very difficult for women to shed the responsibility of their children, even for two hours, in order to pursue their own personal development. Seeing their children happy to leave them, and joining other children in the crêche can be a liberating experience for women. Secondly, by placing emphasis on the need for excellent childcare, you are valuing and respecting the work of the group, and thus valuing participants as individuals.

COFFEE, like biscuits, cannot be ignored if you want to succeed. Freshly ground coffee not only smells wonderful, but again reiterates the value that you give to the group!

CERTIFICATES are important. This doesn't mean that you can only offer a confidence building course if it has some sort of qualification attached to it. In fact, there is no Scotvec Module or Standard Grade. However, if you can design a certificate for your own course and present it to each member at the end, then again you are acknowledging the importance of the step that has been taken. Remember, confidence building may be the first course that many of your group have taken since leaving school.

D is for Desire, Development, Diplomacy

You should only run a confidence building course if you really want to - if you really **d**ESIRE to! You have to be totally convinced, and believe completely that the course you are running will make positive changes in the lives of the women that you will be working with. Facilitators who only run courses because they're told they have to by funders, or who think, "This is fashionable - I'll give it a try," will FAIL because their hearts won't be 100% in what they're doing.

DEVELOPMENT cannot be ignored. This means continually evaluating and developing your course, making changes and trying out new exercises constantly. Our motto is, "Yes! Re-invent the wheel!". Development also relates to your own personal development. Don't sit back thinking that you don't need to work on yourself just because you're facilitating a confidence building course. All the more reason for you to immerse yourself in new books and tapes.

DIPLOMACY is an essential skill required by all good facilitators. Group dynamics are well covered in other books. All we want to say is to be aware of the different opinions that will emerge within discussions, and make sure you create a safe and non-threatening environment for all members to contribute.

E is for Energy and Evaluation

ENERGISING your group is vital. We feed off each other's moods so it's important that the facilitator's energy is used to positive effect.

EVALUATIONS are one way of finding out how your course is progressing. We usually invite our groups to spend some time in the last session brainstorming their thoughts about the course. We ask them to tell us what's been good and what could have been done differently and so on. We always let them do this exercise anonymously either onto cards or flipchart paper. We, as facilitators, also do the same exercise and feed this back to the group. Evaluations can also take place mid-way through the course if necessary, and are useful in helping you to identify where changes might take place.

F is for Fun and Feedback

FUN IS very important. You can't try to have fun of course, because if you were to try, it just wouldn't be fun, would it? So just let it happen along the way. Nothing builds bonds quicker than a good laugh. And even if it is at the expense of the tutor falling over the flipchart stand yet again, have a laugh at yourself - it's worth it!

FEEDBACK isn't only for evaluations. Sometimes in evaluations, women tell you what they think you want to hear, not what they necessarily want to say! So, if you can constantly be aware and listen to the group, you will get the messages loud and clear.

G is for Ground Rules and Games

GROUND RULES are an absolute essential for a group with participants taking part in probably one of the most difficult things they will have to do in their lives. You should never start off the first session with ground rules as this would be a bit heavy. But they should feature as part of an exercise to close the first session. It is up to you how you go about agreeing ground rules in the group. There are many good exercises designed for the purpose (see pages 19 – 63). Don't forget that you are part of the group too, so you should join in the exercise, but do not hog it. Usually you will find that the group will come up with the most important ground rules.

GAMES are an important component of any confidence building course, and there are some crackers in this book. Always be on the look out for ways in which you can adapt children's games, TV games and so on, to fit your course.

H is for Humour, Help and Honesty

There is nothing that will break the ice and bring down barriers quicker than laughter! Never be afraid to inject an element of **h**UMOUR in to your presentation. After all, life's too short to stuff a mushroom!

By **h**ELP we mean co-tutoring. Two heads are better than one, as they say, and when you co-tutor you can energise each other and be twice as productive and creative. Also, if there is a problem, one tutor can deal with it, whilst the other carries on with the group. You will have so much more flexibility when you work with another tutor.

Be yourself at all times. This means being **h**ONEST and brave and getting your group to accept you, warts and all. If this is your first ever confidence building group, then tell them! You are there to learn just as they are. If you can approach your work in this way then you will reap the benefits.

I is for Inspiration and Imagination

INSPIRATION is a wonderful gift which flies in the window and occasionally lands on our shoulders. When it does, don't ignore it, like you have been programmed to do. Acknowledge it, wherever it's come from and make use of it, even if this means that your session has to make a turn around. Remember, inspiration may come to one of the group members also and they deserve the same chance to make use of it too!

IMAGINATION can take you and the group members to places you have never visited before! Using visualisations as a means of building confidence is a very powerful tool. Try it and see for yourself.

J is for Judgement and Jokes

Experience and practice will tell you all you need to know about using your **j**UDGEMENT. How long to give each exercise will vary from group to group, as will the style of delivery which works best for you and so on. Getting in tune with your skills takes time and what a journey you'll have en route!

JOKES: Q. How many men do we need to change a light bulb?
　　　　A. None! We're a confidence building group and we can do it ourselves!!
　　　　(It's OK - yours will be much better than ours!)

K is for Kettle

If you don't have a **k**ETTLE, you won't have a **k**OURSE!

L is for Laughter and Listening

LAUGHTER makes the world go round and your course won't survive without it. See jokes!

The skill of **l**ISTENING to what members of the group are actually saying and not what you think they are saying is a key element to a successful group.

M is for Motivation and Music

MOTIVATION comes from within, some may say, and the facilitator who motivates from without will be successful beyond her wildest dreams!

MUSIC is an inspirational tool which can help set the scene throughout the course. It can be used to motivate members, to energise or relax where appropriate.

N is for Noise

A **n**OISY group is encouraging, no matter what! It means that the members are alive.

O is for Outings

OUTINGS are great. You must make sure that you have enough money in your budget to take the women out at least once. Outings should be decided on by the group as a whole. They should encompass some new experience which the women can take part in. This can range from morning coffee in a very posh hotel to a shoot out at the local Laser Maze. Outings offer an opportunity for people to take on different roles. Tutors can take a back seat, for example, in the organisation of the outing. Outings say, "We value you and the work you are doing," and self-esteem grows as a result.

P is for Personality and Power

As a group facilitator or trainer, you are the **p**ERSON with the responsibility - to begin with anyway. It's your job, whatever your personal feelings, to go to that group and do your stuff. We all have different methods of getting into the right mood or rising to the occasion. It is important to be yourself, always remember you are good enough, and if you don't believe it you need to keep working on it. You will come across a lot of different personality types in a group and as you know, different people like different types of activity. You need to learn not only about moods, but also about personalities, and your own is a good place to start. Share yourself with the group. You can design an exercise to do this. Believe in yourself and believe in them.

P is for **p**OWER too. Don't hold onto the power - give it away! Encourage people to take it. In this way everyone's power is increased. But this involves complete honesty and you might feel a bit vulnerable to start with.

Q is for Quality and Questions

QUALITY should be held up as the kitemark in all aspects of the confidence building course, from the quality of paper used in handouts and exercises, to the quality of attention afforded to each participant.

Encourage **q**UESTIONS - another technique in giving away the power.

R is for Rabbit's Hat

You should always have a **r**ABBIT to pull out of the hat in case you need it. It may be that your session plans go out of the window when only four women turn up instead of ten. Don't waste time mulling over why the others haven't come. There will be a very good reason. Women's lives are very complicated. Just get on and work with those who have turned up. This is when your magic bag comes in useful.

S is for Sabotage, Sabotage, Sabotage!!!

SABOTAGE can be identified by a sinking feeling in the pit of your stomach and is usually accompanied by phrases such as "What's the point of this?", "I just can't think of anything," or "I don't want to do this". It occurs when one, or more likely a pair of participants, disrupt an activity and take on a subversive role. Sabotage can occur for several reasons. It can be caused by a genuine confusion on the part of the participant as to what she is supposed to be doing. In this case, a few minutes taken aside to explain, in a different way, the purpose of the exercise, may be all that is required to set you back on track.. Sabotage can also be caused by participants feeling exposed and outwith their comfort zone. Once more, empathy on the part of the facilitator is needed. Remember, women may be addressing issues in their lives that are very near to the bone. Remind them that it is up to them just how much they want to share with others and at what level they want to take things. Sabotage can also be the result of feeling insecure and maybe even a bit daft! Laughing and giggling, especially in a pair or a small group is sometimes how it shows itself. In this case, it's good to approach the perpetrators with a smile and invite them to share the joke. This gives them the chance to express what they are feeling and have it acknowledged by everyone else. It also means the group as a whole can show them support at the same time and encourage them to continue the activity.

T is for Timing, Tea and Tapes

Before you start any kind of training you must pay special attention to **t**IMING. You must work out the best times for your group considering their lifestyles and responsibilities. Think about the best times for doing such demanding training. Mornings are good. Most people have high energy levels in the mornings. You need to think ahead and plan how you will break the time up so you can get the best out of people. You need to consider the length of exercises and how this equates to the number of women you are working with. For example, it will take twice as long with ten women as it will with five, if the exercise has a feedback component.

TEA - need we say more?!

TAPES are a brilliant resource, whether an inspiring piece of music that you use as a stimulus, or a soothing relaxation tape. Music is a powerful anchor. Video tapes can also be used to good effect too. For example, to illustrate the issues around women's self-image you can look at examples of women on TV.

C is for **C**onfidence

U is for Understanding

UNDERSTANDING means having empathy with the members of the group. It is so important to hold onto unconditional positive regard (although it can sometimes be extremely difficult!) and it is only by doing so that we can bring a human face to our work.

V is for Versatility

No matter how carefully you plan a session and no matter how well prepared you think you are, there will always be a time when something happens that throws all your great ideas into disarray. This is where **V**ERSATILITY comes in. Don't be afraid to let go of your timetable and veer off track if it feels like the right thing to do. It's better to throw caution to the wind and try something different than to stick with a set-in-stone formula that just isn't going to work!

W is for Wonderful Women

WORKING with **W**OMEN on a confidence building course is such an energising experience. You'll share laughs, jokes, confidences and tears. It will all be worthwhile.

X is for Xmas

Always remember that any course you run should wind down or preferably finish, before the start of December. Women usually have the bulk of stuff to do in the run up to **X**MAS and numbers in your group may start to dwindle the nearer you get to the 25th!!

Y is for You and Ylang, Ylang

YOU have such a wonderful opportunity in running a confidence building course, for you have the chance to work on yourself as you work through the sessions!

YLANG, **Y**LANG is a lovely aromatherapy oil for inducing a state of relaxation. We also like lavender. And if you want to zap some energy into the atmosphere then try rosemary or orange and geranium. Or better still, experiment and find out which oils work best for your group.

Z is for Zany

THE **Z**ANIER you are, the more enthused your group will become (honestly!!) and you'll discover that infection can be wonderful!!!

Step by Step Exercises for Confidence Building

Stage One

Icebreakers For All Seasons

Icebreakers are simple exercises which take the pressure off being in a group for what may be the first time since school days. Their purpose is to encourage participation, to motivate and to help participants get to know one another. Make them light and fun. Take time with icebreakers especially over the feedback. Remember, it's the process that's important.

Paired Introductions

Introduce yourself to your partner and find out who she is.

Feedback to whole group with each pair introducing each other - "Hi, I'd like to introduce my partner. This is Shirley," and so on around the group.

or try this

Find out who your partner is and another three things about her. Choose one of those things to tell the group when you introduce her.

or this

Find out who your partner is and what makes her unique - (e.g. a mole shaped like a rabbit).

or even this

Find out who your partner is and something a bit quirky about her - (e.g. she's a Trekky).

or you could try

Find out who your partner is and something that you each have in common (lack of confidence not allowed).

or

Find out who your partner is and what she had for tea last night.

Alphabet Names

Introduce yourself saying something you like which begins with the same letter as your name - e.g. "My name is Laura and I like lollipops!". Ask each participant to introduce herself in this way.

or try this

As each person takes their turn, they introduce all the previous people - e.g. "My name is Laura and I like lollipops. This is Sylvia and she likes silk."

or this

With a small group, or just to keep things going, you can continue this game by doing a second round - e.g. "My name is Laura and I like lollipops, and I hate lupins.".

or else

Let your imagination go, and play around with this basic idea. You could begin with everyone saying something they liked beginning with the letter A, B and so on.

?eman ruoy s'tahW

Getting people moving around and feeling comfortable about sharing information is essential. This activity does both. Each group member is asked to write their name on the flipchart backwards! Each participant then introduces themselves backwards. This is fun and takes away worries people have about their names, or themselves, because they are so concerned about the backward instruction. Use your skills to judge how this is going and how comfortable people are with this. Remember to keep the tempo fast and furious because confusion and hilarity is the aim.

 ?eman ruoy s'tahW

Write your name here

Now write it backwards

or

How about walking backwards as well as writing and speaking backwards!

or else

Try writing with your non dominant hand - (this is a real leveller).

or

Begin with first names only, but as the weeks progress, you could ask participants to write their second names and addresses.

Lion, Eagle, Elephant and Lamb

Ask participants to consider which of these animals they feel themselves to be most like. Once they have had a chance to think, tell them to go and find the others in the group who have chosen the same animal as them. Tell them to talk about what it means to them to be like a Lion, Eagle, Elephant or Lamb. Share feedback with the whole group.

or try this

You could replace the Lion, Elephant, Eagle and Lamb, with other role models - e.g. the cast of a well-known soap opera.

or even this

After participants have done the first part of the exercise - "What do you feel you are most like?" - ask them if they would prefer to be like something else.

or else if your group are feeling really brave

When you ask participants to find their sister animals tell them that they cannot speak but must communicate initially in the appropriate language - e.g. lion - roar.

"I hate that lamp!"

This activity is about encouraging participants to take ownership of their environment, starting with the room you are meeting in now! All you do, is invite people to change something about the room. They might want to move the seating around a bit, or move their seating position. People will find this unusual at first, and may need a little encouragement. (This is your job.)

or try this

If changing things around in a room is a problem, you could bring along some items which make the room more yours during the course, and use these for this exercise.

or else

Ask members to bring something along which they would like to leave in the room for the duration of the course - no family heirlooms please.

or

Have one object, (something symbolic perhaps) which the participants take it in turns to position somewhere in the room at the start of each session.

Ground Rules

Ground rules are important for keeping any group on the right track. They are also essential if you want to measure your progress and prevent yourself from getting stuck.

Cards for Hopes & Fears

Give out two sets of blank cards - one headed 'hopes' and the other 'fears'. Ask each participant to jot down any hopes or fears they may have about the course. The cards are then read out and written on the flipchart by the facilitator. The whole group then designs ground rules to deal with the hopes and fears of the group. Important - these are group ground rules, and responsibility for them does not lie with the facilitator alone.

or you could

Keep the hopes and fears anonymous by putting them into a hat, mixing them up and having them read out in turn round the group.

or else

Hopes and fears cards can be replaced by, 'best group' 'worst group' cards.

or even

Brainstorm, "What do we want from this group?" "What don't we want from this group?"

Have a copy of the ground rules made up for each member of the group, and don't be afraid to get them out for a review from time to time.

Stage Two

Where Am I Now?

It is very important to be able to measure progress, not just for the group as a whole but for the individuals within it and for you the facilitator. This can be achieved by using very simple, yet challenging 'scene setting' exercises, like the one below. Once you have decided that the individuals in the group are ready, try out the exercise below with them, but do it for yourself now!

One Line Description

Write a one line description of yourself which captures exactly how you feel about yourself, right now. It is not for anyone else to see so you can be as honest as you want. Fold it up and put it away. Remember, personal growth comes out of personal challenge and honesty, so go for it.

I am.. .. ..

Photocopy the page overleaf to use with your group →

One Line Description

Write a brief description of yourself here. This is your starting point and you are going to use it as a measure of your success. Take some time to think and try to say exactly what you feel. You may prefer to jot down some words rather than a sentence, or you may even want to draw a picture of yourself. Be as creative as you want and do it now!

I am

What is Confidence?

It's now time to get to the heart of what your course is about - Confidence. Confidence means different things to different people and it's always a good idea to start by finding out what it means to your group. Give them the handout, What Is Confidence? and time to jot down their initial ideas. Then have a lively brainstorm to the flipchart. You could ask people to write their own ideas up on the flipchart - a good confidence building activity.

The group then works on its own definition of confidence. In pairs discuss the handout, What Does Confidence Mean To Me? Each pair then joins with another to work on a definition and so on until the whole group has agreed and is happy with a working definition. (You may end up with a few definitions and that's OK.)

What is important about this activity is that the group begins to examine confidence in an objective way. For the first time, for many people, this thing called confidence is being taken under control by them and not the other way around. It's a small shift but it really is the beginning of the landslide. Take as much time as you need for these exercises. Remember it's the process which is important here.

Photocopy the page overleaf to use with your group ⇾

What Is Confidence?

Take a few moments to jot down your ideas.

What Does Confidence Mean To Me?

Work with a partner to get a definition of confidence.

Who Am I?

Part of the confidence building process is to encourage participants to become comfortable with exploring their own identity. This is why we have included several exercises which help participants become more objective and scientific even when considering themselves. We all have and do many things but they do not define who we are. For example, I am 44 years old but that tells you nothing about who I am. So, do this next exercise for yourself, and use it with your group if you choose. Encourage people to see that we are not the things we have or the things we have done.

Ask participants to answer the following questions, then share in pairs and finish with a whole group discussion - (Well, is that who you are?)

Photocopy the page overleaf to use with your group →

Who am I?

I am

I want

I have

I believe

I feel

I think

I enjoy

I care about

I love

I can

Who's Living My Life Anyway?

The following exercises aim to de-victimise participants and to look at some external factors which lead to a lack of confidence.

Everyday Situations

In groups of four, brainstorm every day situations on a piece of flipchart paper:

e.g.   Going to the shops

          Looking after the kids

          Phoning up the council

Divide them into two lists -

          Situations where we feel confident

          Situations where we don't feel confident

Take some time to unpick the component parts of these situations to discover the elements that go into feeling confident:

e.g.   Familiarity

          Knowledge

          Repetition

Feedback and discussion.

Photocopy the page overleaf to use with your group →

My Story Version One

Write a one page autobiography. Write for five minutes non-stop. It doesn't matter what you write, just keep the pen moving across the page.

Today is   and my life is

What's In A Name?

Work individually, then in pairs.

What is your full name?

How was your name chosen?

What does it mean?

Do you like it?

What does it say about you?

What goes along with having this name?

What is positive about having this name?

What is negative about having this name?

If you could change your name, what would you change it to and why?

Whole group feedback and discussion.

Stage Three
Rewriting the Script

The following exercises help participants to get at the real truth and develop self awareness

The Most Confident Woman

This exercise allows participants to understand their own socialisation processes and can be very revealing. Keeping things light and fun, encourage them to draw and experiment with no holds barred. Once completed, allow plenty of time for all the participants to feedback their ideas. Make sure you give them a chance to change their minds as they begin to realise what they are expressing. Do this exercise for yourself first and you will have a clearer understanding of what may occur.

After the first feedback, ask participants to go into groups of about three to work on a list of the true qualities of confidence. Write the qualities down on cards.

In the whole group, ask participants to give out their cards to people in the group whom they feel already have that particular quality, saying why. This is a wonderful, empowering exercise and should be given adequate time. If you cannot finish this process in one session, carry it over to the next.

Photocopy the page overleaf to use with your group

The Most Confident Woman

Working on your own to begin with take some time to design your most confident woman. She may be a real woman or she could be a combination of ideas you put together. Take a piece of flipchart and be creative.

What does she look like?

What are her clothes like?

What does she sound like?

How does she act?

What does she smell like?

Do you like her?

Why?

Do you want to be like her?

Why?

Visualisation

Confidence is a state. It's a way of feeling and behaving, and everyone will have felt it at some time, in some situation or other, in their lives. When we say we have lost our confidence, that is exactly what we mean. It has not gone off and left us. It's just that we have misplaced it, and find it difficult to call up that state of being. The brief visualisation below is one way of reminding ourselves what that confident state feels like, bringing it into our present lives. Don't be nervous about reading a relaxation script or guided visualisation. We are constantly influenced subconsciously by advertising and the socialisation process. You will be leading an exercise which consciously aims to assist the group to get in touch with feelings of confidence, and bring them out of the past and into the present.

Tell the group what you plan to do and check out how people feel. Make sure that you are going to have peace and quiet for the duration of the exercise (about 20 minutes). You may like to have some soothing music playing in the back-ground as you read the script.

Read the script very slowly, leaving time for participants to get to work on the suggestions that you are making to them. Do not try to make it sound exciting. It's probably better to err on the side of being monotone and boring. That leaves it up to the individuals to have their own experience, which is what you want. If you can get someone to read this to you first, all the better.

Visualisation Script

Close your eyes and relax and begin to become aware of your breathing. As you breathe in and out become aware of how you begin to feel more and more relaxed. As you breathe in and out begin to become aware of how more and more open and relaxed you feel. You may feel a sense of anticipation of the wonderful relaxed sensations you are about to experience, and as you breathe gently and effortlessly in and out you will bring yourself to a place of readiness, a place where you know that everything is well for you and everything is ready. Relax now and let your mind drift away to a time and a place where you experienced those feelings of relaxation and confidence. Take a little time now, to fill up with those feelings and really get in touch with them. Remember how it felt to feel supremely confident. As you re-experience these feelings of confidence imagine that you have a little control sitting attached to your right thumb and first finger and that when you press the control together you can increase the intensity of these feelings. Try that now and check out how it feels. Good. Now you are going to drift forward in time to a time in the future when you know that you want to feel more confident. When you arrive there take a little time to look around, seeing what you will see when you are there - the people who will be there, and how are you feeling now that you are there. Now, become aware of the little control which you have on your right thumb and forefinger and press them together and check out how that feels. Yes. Good. Take some time now to try out your control in a few other locations in the future. Now, in your own time, begin to be aware of noises and the people in the room around you. Now, bring yourself back to awareness, bringing with you all those feelings of confidence and composure, ready to talk about your experience with the rest of the group. You're feeling ready now to come back, and as I count to three, you will wake up bright and enthusiastic. One, two, three, welcome back!

Role Models (1)
Who Are Yours?

Who are the three women you most look up to?

1.

2.

3.

Why do you look up to these women?

1.

2.

3.

How have your role models affected your life?

1.

2.

3.

Work individually, then in pairs.

Whole group feedback.

Try to identify the common characteristics.

Role Models (2)
Who Are Yours?

Who are the three people you most look up to?

1.

2.

3.

Why do you look up to these people?

1.

2.

3.

How have your role models affected your life?

1.

2.

3.

Work individually, then in pairs.

Whole group feedback.

Try to identify the common characteristics.

The Most Confident You!

Individually, in pairs and then whole group feedback.

After some work on what confidence means to us, we sometimes become clearer about what we really need to change in order to become more confident. Redesign the most confident you. Acknowledge the qualities you have and the ones you would like to awaken within you.

The qualities I know I have.   The qualities I want to have.

My Story Version Two

Write another one page autobiography. This time get in touch with your deepest feelings and let go of all your inhibitions. Don't stop and think. Just let your writing come straight from the heart. Do not edit anything. If you feel angry, let it out! Write for five minutes non-stop.

Today is   and my life is

Change Is Inevitable

The following exercises aim to demystify and take the fear out of change. This is really important to think about. It's all very well to sit and think, "I want to be different. Things have to change. It's time for a change." But what are the implications of change? Many of us are frightened of change because we are afraid of the unknown. This fear can have a crippling effect and hold us back from exciting and thrilling opportunities.

The important thing to remember is, whether we are frightened or not, change will happen. Believe it or not, change is probably the most constant aspect of our lives.

OK, not all change feels good. However, if we can deal with change in a positive way, our lives will be much healthier and happier.

You may feel like you are stuck in a rut and that nothing is changing in your life. What we need to be aware of is that change happens in lots of different ways. All the time. Some changes are sudden, like death or redundancy. Some changes are gradual, like ageing. All change affects us in one way or another.

Comfort Zones

Comfort Zones are where we think it's safest to be. They are the places we know well. They are the people and kinds of people we have always got on with. They are the things we do because we have always done them. They are the way we do things because that's the way we've always done them. They are the most destructive force in personal growth. Where would we all be now if people hadn't ventured outside their comfort zones to try something new? Still sitting in a cave somewhere no doubt. Doing things differently is not easy, especially if we haven't done this for a long time. So, if you want to encourage people to try this, remember to start with small steps and simple exercises.

Comfort Zones Exercise

In pairs, everyone stands up.

Tell participants,

"Your partner is allowed to ask you to change something about your appearance, e.g. move your watch from one hand to the other, then you do the same. That's it. Sit down, in a different seat from the one you left."

Discuss how involuntary change felt.

Change Gets Easier With Practice

Ask the group to work in pairs to help each other identify something that they could change, just for the sake of it. Encourage them to go for it! Feedback in next session.

Messages From The Past

In the process of building confidence, women are often given unhelpful messages. The next exercise allows participants to explore the negative messages which others have given them. On completion, the group should discuss the underlying message in what others have said to them. There should then be a symbolic 'scoring out' of the old messages before participants develop new positive messages for themselves.

Photocopy the page overleaf to use with your group

Messages From The Past

Write a list of the messages you have received about how to be you.

What my mum said

What my dad said

What the family said

What my teachers said

What my friends said

What work said

Messages For Now!

Write a list of the things that you would like to tell them about you now!

Message for my mum

Message for my dad

Message for the family

Message for my teachers

Message for my friends

Message for work

Exercise For Change (1)

Think about times in your life when change has occurred.

Choose one change which was a good experience and one change which was not so good.

My good experience was

Were you responsible for this change?

How did you incorporate this change into your life?

What did you learn about yourself because of this change?

Are you glad that the change happened?

Could you have done anything to prevent the change?

Would you change anything if you could?

Is there any unfinished business that you need to deal with concerning this change?

Can you do anything about this now?

If you were advising a dear friend what would you say about the way they dealt with this change?

Exercise For Change (2)

My not so good experience of change was

Were you responsible for this change?

How did you incorporate this change into your life?

What did you learn about yourself because of this change?

Are you glad that the change happened?

Could you have done anything to prevent the change?

Would you change anything if you could?

Is there any unfinished business that you need to deal with concerning this change?

Can you do anything about this now?

If you were advising a dear friend what would you say about the way they dealt with this change?

Questions For Making Changes

What do you want?

What are the things you want to move towards?

What are the things you want to move away from?

Who are the people who will be part of what you want?

Who are the people you will leave behind to move towards what you want?

What will you have to admit to yourself before you get what you want?

What are you afraid of?

Will staying afraid lead to you getting what you want?

Do you want what you want enough, to change?

Stage Four
Strategies for Confidence

The following exercises aim to give participants strategies for building confidence and a more positive culture.

Affirmations

Now that we have begun to acknowledge the external factors which have an effect on our confidence, it's time to do some more work on our perception of ourselves. "Ten Things I Like About Myself" is a good place to start. It dispels our tendency to think we are unlikeable. It also introduces the idea that we are responsible for how we feel about things and that includes ourselves. Whatever you think about yourself, you will live your life attempting to fulfil that prophesy. So why not think of yourself in a kinder light.

The complementary exercise, "Ten Things Others Like About Me," will assist participants in their change of perspective. This can be done in the group or may be taken away to do with friends and family.

Affirmations are positive statements designed to enable participants to get what they want - i.e. to feel more confident. You can work as a group to gather together a collection of affirmations, as well as encouraging individuals to go away and work on their own personal affirmations.

Use any opportunity to repeat positive affirmations during the group sessions. The more often these positive things are said, the more likely it is that people will begin to accept positive change.

Photocopy the pages overleaf to use with your group →

Ten Things I Like About Myself

Don't think about this exercise too long. Just get on and do it!

1.

2.

3.

4.

5.

6.

7.

8.

9.

10.

Ten Things Others Like About Me

Go to other members of the group or take this home and chose supportive people to help you with this task.

1.

2.

3.

4.

5.

6.

7.

8.

9.

10.

Positive Affirmations

The most common positive affirmation and one of the most difficult to say into a mirror without laughing is the one that goes, *"I like myself."*

Go round the group and let everyone give this a try. Now go and work in pairs to get a few more.

1.

2.

3.

4.

5.

6.

7.

8.

9.

10.

Give Yourself A Treat

This is an important part of the process in beginning to value yourself in a new way, so don't be tempted to miss it out. Work in pairs.

Think of one way in which you can give yourself a treat.

1. How are you going to treat yourself?

2. When will you do this thing?

3. Why are you giving yourself a treat?

After the treat

1. Were you successful?

2. How did it feel?

3. Why did you give yourself a treat?

4. Are you worth a treat?

5. What will be your next treat to yourself and why?

A Letter To Myself

Imagine that you are your very best friend and you want to write a letter (to you) to support you in your journey forward.

Dear

Positive Input Data Bank

Hand out a sheet to everyone.

Tell the group, *"Write down the name of the person on your right and underneath write something positive about that person. Pass the sheet of paper to the left and continue until everyone has the sheet with their name on it."*

Photocopy the page overleaf to use with your group ⇒

Positive Input Data Bank

Name.. .. ..

Input.. .. ..

Input.. .. ..

Input.. .. ..

Input.. .. ..

Input.. .. ..

Input.. .. ..

Input.. .. ..

Input.. .. ..

Input.. .. ..

Input.. .. ..

Input.. .. ..

Input.. .. ..

Input.. .. ..

Input.. .. ..

A Slogan For The Group.

In small groups work on the questions below to help you create a slogan for your group.

1. What is important to the people in this group?

2. What do you want to say about yourselves?

3. What do you want others to know about you?

4. What is the message you get from the answers above?

5. Can you turn it into something really catchy?

Our slogan is

Ten Things I Want To Do Before I Die!

We all have hopes and dreams and inner desires, but often everyday life gets in the way and we never quite make it. If you knew a child who had a dream, a dream that made them pink with excitement, would you encourage them in their dreams or not? What if you had a second chance to go for the things you wanted to go for? Well you have and it all starts here!

Go for it!

Make a list of ten things you want to do before you die. **Now!**

1.

2.

3.

4.

5.

6.

7.

8.

9.

10.

Turning Dreams Into Wishes Into Reality

Chose one of the ten things from the previous exercise and work on these questions to make it come true.

What is your dream?

Do you really believe that you deserve to have this thing?

Does your dream have more than one step to make it come true?

What is the very first step towards your dream?

Now write it as if it was all set up and really happening and you are telling someone about it:

How does this dream fit in with the rest of your life? Do you need to tell other people? Will it affect other people? Do you feel OK about how it's going to affect others?

What things do you need to make this happen?

If you don't have them all, where can you begin to gather the things you need?

What do you get by not following your dream?

What is the very first step you will take?

When will you take it?

Good luck! You have set the wheels in motion. Just continue with this process and watch what happens.

Stage Five
Rounds for All Occasions

Rounds are good for starting, finishing and checking things out.

Take it in turns to go around the group, each member ending the statement:

Something that **surprised** me about today was.. .. ..

Something that **pleased** me about today was.. .. ..

Something that **confused** me about today was.. .. ..

Something that **delighted** me about today was.. .. ..

Something that **niggled** me about today was.. .. ..

Something that **tickled** me about today was.. .. ..

Something that **challenged** me about today was.. .. ..

Something that **bugged** me about today was.. .. ..

Something that **excited** me about today was.. .. ..

Reviewing and Ending
Warm Fuzzy Feelings

Compliments

Everyone in the group gets a pile of stickers on which they must write a complimentary statement about everyone else in the group. These are then stuck on the backs of the appropriate group members. This is done simultaneously, so people are milling around slapping each other on the back. When everyone is done, you take it in turns for a partner to peel off the stickers and read them out loud to the rest of the group.

Why I Really, Really Haven't Been Behaving Confidently!

This is a simple yet powerful review process. Give the group this question and ask participants to work in pairs to find their answer. Feedback to whole group.

One Line Description

Get out the one line descriptions people did at the start of the course and do the exercise again. Invite people to share if they wish.

Leaving On A High!

Create an elevated spot in the room and invite participants one by one to take their place on high, to address the group. They are received with tumultuous applause.

Symbolic Gift

Use an object as a symbol - e.g. a flower or an ornament. Each participant gives another the gift saying why they want to give the other a gift. The object is passed round until everyone has received and given the gift.

For The Facilitator Who Has Not Been Paired Up With Anyone!

Why not give the group a chance to find out a bit more about you by offering them a 20 question session (if you are brave enough).

Now That You Are More Confident

The following exercise may appear to have a rather unusual language pattern. This is intentional. The series of questions firstly begins to induce a state of feeling more confident. As the questions progress, the state of confidence is given context, and the participants can begin to see themselves in a positive light in a variety of future situations. Remembering that we all work hard to fulfil our own expectations, this exercise increases the likelihood of positive experiences in the future. The phrase, 'You Are More Confident' appears several times throughout the question sheet, and acts as an affirmation of external expectation.

Photocopy the page overleaf to use with your group ⤳

Now That You Are More Confident

Do the exercise in pairs, feedback and discuss in the whole group.

Answer these questions.

1. What does it feel like to be more confident?

2. What is the first thing you will do now that you feel more confident?

3. How will you behave now that you are more confident?

4. Who are the kinds of people that you will spend your time with now that you are more confident?

5. Where are the places you will go now that you are more confident?

6. How does it feel now to be more confident?

Letting Go

Read this short story and as you read it, think about the baggage that the heroine is carrying with her. Try to identify what she needs to let go, to get on with the rest of her life.

"Cinderella had been living happily ever after for about two years now. She seemed to have everything that she wanted. She had lovely dresses and went to balls a lot with Prince Charming. The thing was though, the Prince was away quite a lot and she spent most of the time in the palace wandering about on her own. The magical stuff that used to be such fun was gone forever. No mice being turned into coachmen and no pumpkin coaches. Life seemed very predictable and she felt she had no important part to play. She felt that she couldn't really do anything, but clean up the kitchen and stuff like that. She wasn't sure about the people who came to the palace to visit her. They were very pleasant and all that, but did they really like her or was it just that she was rich and famous? She thought about her old family too from time to time, and when she did she felt so guilty about what had happened to them. They were all living in another country now and they were never allowed to return. It is true that they had been particularly mean to her, especially that last attempt to throw her out of the palace tower on the morning of her wedding. But she still felt guilty. Besides, life was not boring when they were around."

Cinderella was unhappy and she didn't know why.
Cinderella wanted to do something but she didn't know what.
Can you help her?

Discuss.

1. What changes, if any, have you become aware of in yourself or in your behaviour since you began your confidence building course?

2. In which areas of your life do you feel most confident now?

3. In which situations do you need more practice in being confident?

4. What are the three most important things that you have learned about yourself during this course?

What did you like most about the course?

What did you like least about the course?

What is the most important thing you learned during the course?

What would you say to other people about the course?

Would you say your confidence has increased during the course?

Would you make any changes to the course?

Feel The Fear and Do it Anyway, **Susan Jeffers**, Arrow Books

I'm OK, You're OK, **Thomas A Harris**, Pan Books

Staying OK, **A & T Harris**, Pan Books

Psycho Cybernetics, **Maxwell Maltz**, Wiltshire Book Co.

A Woman In Your Own Right, **Anne Dickson**, Quartet Books

Women Who Run With The Wolves, **Clarissa Pinkola Estes**, Rider Books

Mother Wit, **Diana Mariechild**, Crossing Press

Living Magically, **Gill Edwards**, Piatkus Books